SEQUENCES OF EARTH & SPACE

Seasons

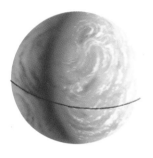

Andres Llamas Ruiz

Illustrations by Luis Rizo

Sterling Publishing Co., Inc.
New York

Illustrations by Luis Rizo
Text by Andres Llamas Ruiz
Translated by Natalia Tizón

Library of Congress Cataloging-in-Publication Data

Llamas Ruiz, Andrés.
    [Estaciones. English]
    Seasons / Andres Llamas Ruiz.
        p.   cm. — (Sequences of earth & space)
    Includes index.
    Summary: An illustrated introduction to what the seasons are,
why and when they change, and how they affect plants, animals,
and people.
    ISBN 0-8069-9335-9
    1. Seasons—Juvenile literature. [1. Seasons.] I. Title. II.
Series: Llamas Ruiz, Andrés.   Secuencias de la tierra y el espa-
cio. English.
    QB637.4.L6413   1996
    508—dc20
                                                 96–9197
                                                 AC

1   3   5   7   9   10   8   6   4   2

Published by Sterling Publishing Company, Inc.
387 Park Avenue South, New York, N.Y. 10016
Originally published in Spain by Ediciones Estes
©1996 by Ediciones Estes, S.A. ©1996 by Ediciones Lema, S.L.
English version and translation © 1996 by Sterling Publishing Company, Inc.
Distributed in Canada by Sterling Publishing
℅ Canadian Manda Group, One Atlantic Avenue, Suite 105
Toronto, Ontario, Canada M6K 3E7
Distributed in Great Britain and Europe by Cassell PLC
Wellington House, 125 Strand, London WC2R 0BB, England
Distributed in Australia by Capricorn Link (Australia) Pty Ltd.
P.O. Box 6651, Baulkham Hills, Business Centre, NSW 2153, Australia

Sterling ISBN 0-8069-9335-9

Contents

The Earth and the Sun

Seasons are caused as the earth travels around the sun; as the position of the earth's surface changes—moving either closer to or away from the sun—the seasons change. Similarly, during its daily movements, the earth spins around the sun, and night turns to day.

If you look at the sky during the day, the sun appears to be traveling from east to west, but this is not true. It is the earth that moves, rotating on its axis once every 24 hours.

Because of this movement, it is daytime for the part of the earth's surface that is facing the sun and nighttime when the earth rotates hiding the same area from the sun.

While the earth rotates on its own, it also moves around the sun in an elliptical path. This movement is called a revolution. It is a long journey—one that lasts 365 days. As the earth revolves, weather conditions change periodically. These changes cause the seasons.

At the same time that the earth revolves around the sun, it rotates on its own. The earth's axis is not parallel to the sun; instead, it tilts, so that when the sun's rays hit the earth's northern half (the northern hemisphere) directly, they hit the southern half (the southern hemi-sphere) indirectly. This explains why, when it is summer in the northern hemisphere, it is winter in the south, and vice-versa.

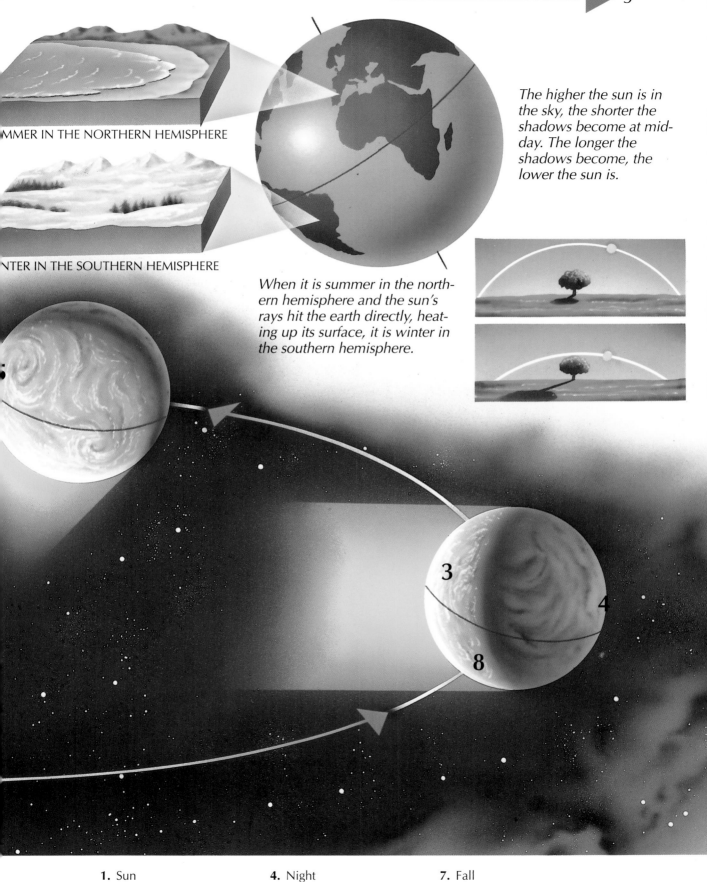

MMER IN THE NORTHERN HEMISPHERE

NTER IN THE SOUTHERN HEMISPHERE

The higher the sun is in the sky, the shorter the shadows become at mid-day. The longer the shadows become, the lower the sun is.

When it is summer in the north-ern hemisphere and the sun's rays hit the earth directly, heat-ing up its surface, it is winter in the southern hemisphere.

1. Sun	**4.** Night	**7.** Fall
2. Earth's orbit	**5.** Spring	**8.** Winter
3. Day	**6.** Summer	

January

There are 365 days, 52 weeks, 12 months, and four seasons in a year.

January is the first month of the year. During this month, it is winter in the northern hemisphere and the days in certain regions are short and cold. This is because the sun's rays hit the surface at a very low angle.

You can see the sun very low on the horizon, illuminating and dispersing heat over a large area. Even when it shines at midday, its rays are not strong enough to warm up the area.

At the beginning of the month, the sun rises relatively late in the morning and sets early in the evening. We already know that the earth changes its position continuously, relative to the sun, and that is why during this month, sunlight hours become 1 minute longer each morning and half a minute longer each afternoon.

Nature rests in silence. Very little can grow during this season and life is very difficult for all. Snow covers the landscape, the trees rest, and the lakes and creeks freeze over many times. In January, most plants are still "asleep," but some, like the almond tree, start to bloom.

Animals must protect themselves from the cold. If it has snowed, the food they must search for may be covered by the snow. Most insects either sleep or die during the cold winter. Some go underground or stay inside their own cocoons, waiting for the spring.

1

In the winter, some animals live beneath a protective blanket of snow and ice. For example, under the ice, water maintains a temperature of 39°F (4°C), even though the temperature above may be several degrees below zero. This allows fish to survive the cold.

Snow is beneficial. It acts as a blanket by protecting the ground from the cold and preventing the earth from freezing.

January, the sun's rays hit the earth at such an gle that they distribute their energy over a eater area than they do in summer; this means ey do not carry enough heat to warm up the vironment.

The movement of the stars is caused by the earth's rotation. You can see here the starry sky of a winter night in the northern hemisphere.

1. Ice covers the surface of lakes and ponds; since it is not as dense as water, it floats.

2. Deciduous trees wait for the end of winter with their branches bare of leaves.

3. Many animals stop their activity and spend their winter in hibernation.

February

February is the shortest month of the year. It has only 28 days, except every fourth year (leap year), when it has 29 days.

Why are there 29 days in February every 4 years? There is a very simple explanation. During its long journey around the sun, the earth does not take exactly 365 days to complete one revolution, but 365 days and 6 hours!

As you may have guessed, those 6 hours accumulate, and every 4 years they add one more day—24 hours—to February. Although a year may seem like a long time to spend going around the sun, do not think that the earth moves slowly. Actually, our planet moves in space at a speed of 66,340 miles (107,000 km) per hour.

In February, the winter cold continues, but during this month the hours of sunlight are 1 minute and 45 seconds longer each morning and afternoon.

In the forests, the branches of deciduou trees are completely bare of leaves, and mo animals continue to rest. However, the increase in sunlight hours indicates that spring is approaching.

During the month of February, the sun's rays that reach the earth's surface are very weak, since the sun is still very low on the horizon. Despite this, the weather is not as cold as it was earlier in the winter.

The earth has been orbiting the sun. In February, the sun's rays do not strike the earth's surface at such a sharp angle in the northern hemisphere, but it is still winter.

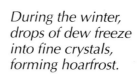

During the winter, drops of dew freeze into fine crystals, forming hoarfrost.

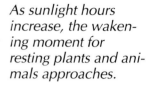

As sunlight hours increase, the wakening moment for resting plants and animals approaches.

1. The ice covering the river begins to melt.

2. The trees' branches cannot hold the weight of the snow; many of them start to show buds.

3. The few lonely birds crossing the sky become more noticeable.

4. The snow begins to melt, exposing patches of green grass growing underneath.

March

March is a very special month, because it foreshadows the end of winter hardships and the beginning of spring.

The nights are still cold, but during the day it is warmer and sunlight hours increase. During this month, daily sunlight hours will increase by 2 minutes every morning and 1 minute and 45 seconds every afternoon.

Everywhere, life gradually wakes up. Birds begin to sing again and the frozen ground starts to thaw. As soon as all the snow and ice melt, life begins again on the forest ground.

March 20 or 21 is the spring equinox in the northern hemisphere. This is a very special day, because it has exactly 12 hours of daylight and 12 of darkness. Each day the sun will continue to rise a little higher in the sky.

Spring weather can be very unstable. There may be sudden showers, and raindrops may even turn into hail.

The movement of the earth makes the sun rise higher in the sky every day. That is how daylight hours increase and the sun's rays create more warmth.

The spring equinox falls on March 20 or 21, when the earth's axis forms an angle with an "imaginary line" that passes through the center of the earth and sun.

Some early blooming plants take part in a race to grow.

In its orbit around the sun, the earth passes through some points more distant than others, but this is not the cause of either summer or winter.

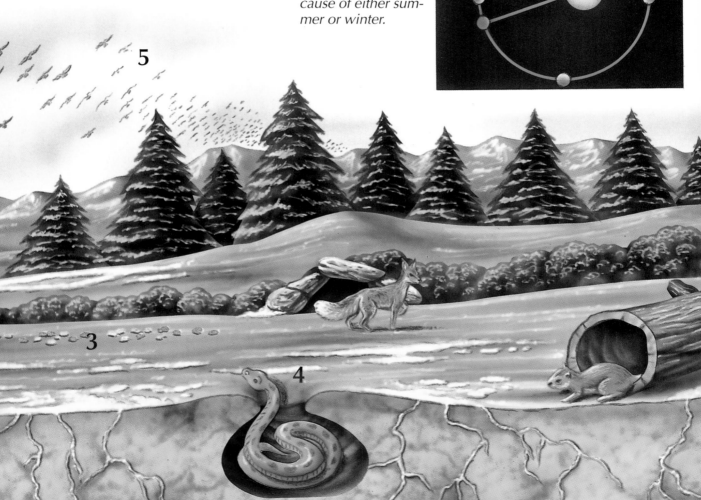

1. A great number of fish swim again under the water's surface.

2. During the thaw, water slowly filters into the ground.

3. Early blooming plants show their multicolored flowers.

4. Some animals awake from their winter rest.

5. Groups of birds begin to cruise the skies.

6. The buds on the trees are ready to open.

April

In the northern hemisphere, April brings more sunlight. During this month, the sun rises earlier than it did in January and sets later. Thanks to the earth's movement, the days become longer by 2 minutes every morning, and 1 minute and 45 seconds every afternoon.

April is a moody month. Some days it may be very hot, because the sun's rays hit the northern hemisphere at a lesser angle. On other days, it can seem as cold as winter. Still, the snow has usually melted and the warm sun will bring many animals out of their winter hiding places. Birds sing all day long, and as soon as they finish building the nests they start laying their eggs.

Plants open themselves to the sun. Their buds swell up until the tiny scales start to separate and little, moist leaves appear. New branches grow longer, searching for sunlight every day they grow new leaves.

Spring is special. Most plants and trees bud, and there are flowers everywhere.

In April, there are more sunlight hours than darkness hours and the weather turns warmer. This is all due to the position of the earth relative to the sun. Finally, it is spring.

The earth's revolution gives the impression that the sun has gradually been rising in the sky during April. The rays strike at a lesser angle, and it is warmer.

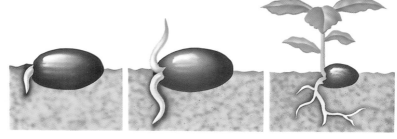

Spring's humidity and heat germinate seeds hidden under fallen leaves. Many of these seeds have spent the winter on the ground.

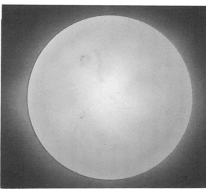

Although April brings more sun, there may still be frost—especially at the beginning of the month—and very cold winds.

1. Many animals now begin to reproduce.

2. Many amphibians' eggs are noticeable under water; on the water's surface, you can see many insects.

3. The trees are beginning to be covered with leaves.

4. Birds build nests.

5. Inside their burrows, some animals have already delivered offspring.

May

During this month, the days become gradually warmer and the nights become shorter.

At the beginning of May, the sun continues to rise earlier in the morning and to set later in the evening. The daylight hours are 1 minute 30 seconds longer each morning and afternoon.

Many plants have blossomed and the fields are filled with color. The trees are growing buds and their new leaves are green and tender. In the spring, plants work tire-lessly and the millions of leaves in the forests create food through photosynthesis. Crickets hide among the plants; the insects' noisy concerts can be heard for hours.

In May, the amount of sun received in the northern hemisphere increases. As you already know, this is due to the angle of the earth's axis relative to its orbit in space.

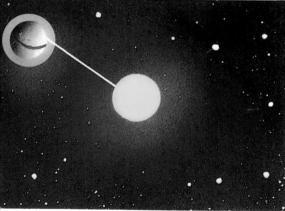

In May, the anticipation of summer is noticeable in the northern hemisphere. The sun's rays reach the ground with increased intensity, covering a smaller area than they did in winter and filling it with more intense heat.

Plants display a wide variety of flowers from competing with one another to attract insects that can pollinate them.

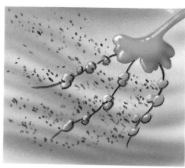

In some cases, pollination is helped by the wind, which carries pollen from one flower to another.

1. The branches of deciduous trees are now covered with leaves, and less light reaches the forest floor.

2. The sun is higher on the horizon.

3. Under water there are many tadpoles.

4. Birds are ready to incubate their eggs.

5. Many insects have already laid their eggs; these are now ready to open.

6. Many butterflies attempt their first flight.

June

Summer starts on June 21. This is the longest day and the shortest night of the year. Days become longer until June 21, when spring ends. This date marks the summer solstice—dawn is very early and the day seems very long. The sun has reached its highest point in the sky; from this day on, sunlight hours will begin to shorten, losing 1 to 2 minutes each morning.

In June, when the sun is high up in the sky, its rays are strong and warm. In clear patches of the forest, the light is bright and temperatures are beginning to rise.

Many grass plants open the tender petals at the top of their slender stems and start to bloom. Their flowers are so small that they do not attract the attention of the insects, but they are pollinated by the wind. During this month many animals are able to eat green, juicy plants. You can also see butterflies emerge from their cocoons and spread their wings.

During this month, each day gets warmer as summer approaches. Summer begins on June 21. On this day, dawn comes very early, the sun reaches its highest point in the sky, and the day seems very long.

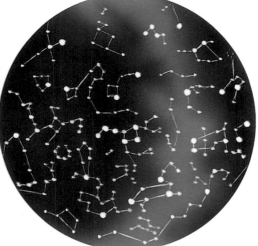

This is how the sky looks at night at the end of spring. You can distinguish some of the most well-known stars and constellations.

June 21 or 22 is the summer solstice. The earth's axis tilts toward the sun at a maximum of 23.5 degrees. On this day, the northern hemisphere receives the most solar radiation!

It takes the earth 24 hours to turn 360 degrees relative to its particular star, the sun.

1. The sun is very high and shines brightly.

2. The branches of many trees are completely covered with blossoms.

3. In their nests, little birds ask for food from their hardworking parents.

4. There are insects everywhere.

5. For hunting animals, this is a time of abundance, but they must concentrate their energy on hunting for their offspring.

July

In July, the summer heat has already arrived. As the sun's rays strike the earth's surface, their angle continues to decrease. The days are very long, with the sun rising very early in the morning and setting late in the evening. During the course of July, however, the days will shorten, losing 1 minute every morning and 1 minute every afternoon.

Often on hot summer days there are storms where a large amount of rain falls in a short period of time, causing dangerous floods. A storm forms this way: During summer's very hot days, the air gets so warm that it becomes very light and rises quickly. As it rises, it seeks out cold air, and its water vapor condenses into little drops that form thick, threatening clouds. As both the cold and hot air masses push and crash against one another, the clouds are charged with electricity, which creates lightning.

2

In July, the sun's rays hit the surface of the earth with great intensity.

The earth's axis forms a 66.5 degree angle relative to the plane of movement around the sun.

In July, it is very hot in the northern hemisphere. This is partly because the oceans retain heat. The position of the planet continues to make the sun appear to be very high on the horizon.

Notice how a summer storm comes closer. It is hot and humid, and some people say that the air is loaded with electricity.

1. The heat, especially at noon (when the sun is high up in the sky), can be suffocating.

2. Almost all nests are empty because even the young birds have learned to fly.

3. The amphibians have completed their metamorphosis and most of them have emerged from the water in their adult form.

4. For the offspring of many species, the adventures outside the safety of their burrows now begin.

August

In August, the heat can be suffocating. The midday sun—high up on the horizon—hardly creates any shadows.

But the fall is inevitably approaching: The days continue to shorten every morning and afternoon.

The summer heat is emphasized by the sun's continuing high position in the sky (during winter the sun will be much lower at the same time and place). As you know, this is because the imaginary axis, around which the earth turns, tilts at an angle.

In August, the days are very hot. The oceans retain heat, as does the dry land.

In August, the days continue to shorten, but it is still very hot.

Shooting stars are grains of dust that move through the solar system, burning up as they enter the earth's atmosphere.

1. At noon, the sun's rays hardly create any shadows.
2. Water levels have decreased from the intense evaporation.
3. Some plants dry up and die.
4. In mid-August, storks are the first birds to leave on their yearly migration.
5. Fruit starts to ripen on the trees.
6. During the warmest hours, many animals rest in the shade.

September

The days shorten and it begins to cool off.

At the beginning of September, the sun rises later in the morning and sets earlier in the evening. Throughout the month, sunlight hours will shorten every morning and afternoon. Finally, autumn will start on September 22 or 23, the day of the fall equinox in the northern hemisphere.

It almost seems that nature has foreseen the change that is approaching. The leaves are not so green anymore and pastures are beginning to turn yellow. Fruits ripen and seeds fall to the ground. Each seed could produce new life, but very few will fall in places that have adequate conditions for germination.

In some cases, the wind will help scatter the seeds. Many seeds have membranes that help them to be carried aloft. Other seeds have fuzz, which looks like a small parachute and allows them to be easily carried by the wind.

There are two equinoxes per year, in the spring and the fall. During an equinox, night and day last exactly the same length of time— 12 hours each.

In the northern hemisphere, September 22 or 23 marks the fall equinox, but it is the beginning of spring in the southern hemisphere. On March 21 or 22 the roles reverse.

From the North Pole, all the stars in the northern hemisphere's sky can be seen.

When the afternoon ends and the sun begins to set, its rays pass through a thicker atmosphere, creating pretty colors.

3

4

. The sun continues to lower in its long journey across the sky.

. The leaves of deciduous trees start to change color.

3. Trees and bushes are covered with fruit.

4. Many animals, such as these squirrels, start to store nuts for the winter.

5. Many insects become less active.

October

At the beginning of October, the sun rises at approximately 6:45 AM and sets at 6:20 PM in the northeast. But the continuous movement of the earth shortens the days, by 1 minute and 45 seconds every morning and 2 minutes every afternoon.

The growing period of the trees is over as they prepare to spend the winter resting. Their leaves turn yellow, red, light green, and brown as they dry up and the wind blows them off the branches. Before the leaves fall, the tree sucks out all their nutrients and stores them in its branches and trunk. In time, the leaves that fall to the ground will become humus. (Sometimes this can take several years.)

In the fall, the forest is full of fruit, which has a double function. Fruit is useful for the reproduction of plants and it also serves as precious food for many animals.

The strength of the sun's rays gradually weakens as they reach the earth's surface.

In October, the sun's rays reach the earth's surface at a larger angle. Because the rays illuminate a larger area than in the summer, their intensity is lessened.

When the leaves are gold and red, they are ready to fall off the trees.

During fall nights, when the ground is cold, water vapor condenses and forms fog.

1. The color of the sky is not so bright as in the summer.

2. Many birds migrate south.

3. Rain and fog are frequent.

4. The leaves of deciduous trees turn color.

5. Large numbers of mushrooms grow on the forest floor.

6. Animals store nuts away for the winter.

November

In November, the days are gray with clouds and fog, and the nights can be very cold. The rigor of the coming winter starts to become noticeable.

At the beginning of the month, the sun rises late and sets early. Sunlight hours are reduced by more than a minute every morning and afternoon.

The earth's movement around the sun causes the northern hemisphere to tilt relative to the sun and the rays lose strength. This is why the days are becoming colder.

By now, most deciduous trees have los their leaves because of the fall storms that force them from their branches. Fir trees, however, keep their needles and continue t perform photosynthesis.

It is colder and darkness comes earlier. In the forest, less sunlight reaches the trees' leaves, which gradually change color. In the end, even the slightest wind wi blow the leaves from the trees.

After a rainy day many mushrooms appear on the ground. They seem to come out of nowhere.

In November, the days gradually shorten. The sunlight hitting the surface of the northern hemisphere is reduced even more and the sun's rays are more indirect every day.

A starry sky on a fall night in the northern hemisphere.

4

3

1. Deciduous trees have dropped almost all of their leaves.

2. Fallen leaves pile up on the ground and decay until they become humus.

3. Most butterflies and beetles only survive until fall.

4. Very few animals, such as this fox, remain active.

December

This month the sun continues to rise late in the morning and to set late in the afternoon; sunlight hours will shorten by 1 minute each morning and afternoon. December 21 or 22 marks the winter solstice in the northern hemisphere—the shortest day of the year and the longest night. This is the first day of winter; from now on, the days will begin to get longer.

During December, the sun passes low on the sky horizon. Every day, the weather gets colder, because the sun's rays weaken daily as they hit the earth's surface. Many mountains are covered with snow.

The bare trees seem dead, but they are not. The ground is covered with snow and very little can grow. It is cold, but the plants and animals of the forest adapt to the hunge and cold of winter. For example, many animals spend the winter sleeping. Other animals, however, are awake, living off the supplies they gathered and put away earlier in the fall.

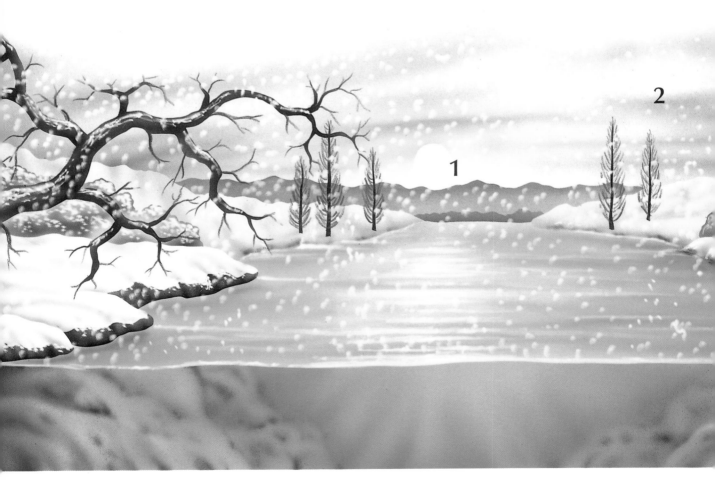

Where are the animals that could be seen everywhere in the spring and the summer? Many of them hide. Snails, for instance, close themselves into the deepest part of their shells, sealing the entrance with a dry coat of mucus. Others, such as mice, continue actively accumulating food to see them through the remaining days of winter.

At sunset, many of the sun's blue rays are scattered in the atmosphere, leaving lights of a dazzling reddish color.

December 21 or 22 is the winter solstice. The earth's axis is at its maximum inclination, and the southern hemisphere is now the most illuminated. The sun's rays reach the northern hemisphere at a very low angle.

The age of a tree is shown by the two new rings formed every year inside the trunk.

1. The sun passes very low on the horizon.

2. The falling snow makes it difficult for animals to hide from their enemies.

3. Some animals must survive by eating the leaves that stick out from under the snow.

4. The dormouse and many other animals prefer to hibernate.

Phases of the Moon

During the year, the seasons are not the only things that change. Every month, you can notice major changes in the amount of visible moon surface. These are the phases of the moon. The moon is the earth's only natural satellite. You have already seen that the earth revolves around the sun, but our planet is also the center of the moon's movement; it makes one complete revolution around the earth every 27.3 days.

The moon travels around the earth from east to west. When the moon partly passes between the sun and the earth, it is in its "new moon" phase and we are unable to see any illuminated part of it.

The moon then starts "growing," and one week later it is in its "first quarter" phase.

The moon is in the "full" phase exactly one week later, when it is in the position opposite to the one during the new moon phase. At this time, the moon appears to be totally illuminated by the sun's rays.

From this moment on, the illuminated surface that can be seen from the earth becomes smaller every day. This is the "last quarter" phase.

The moon does not have light of its own. It shines because sunlight reflects off its surface.

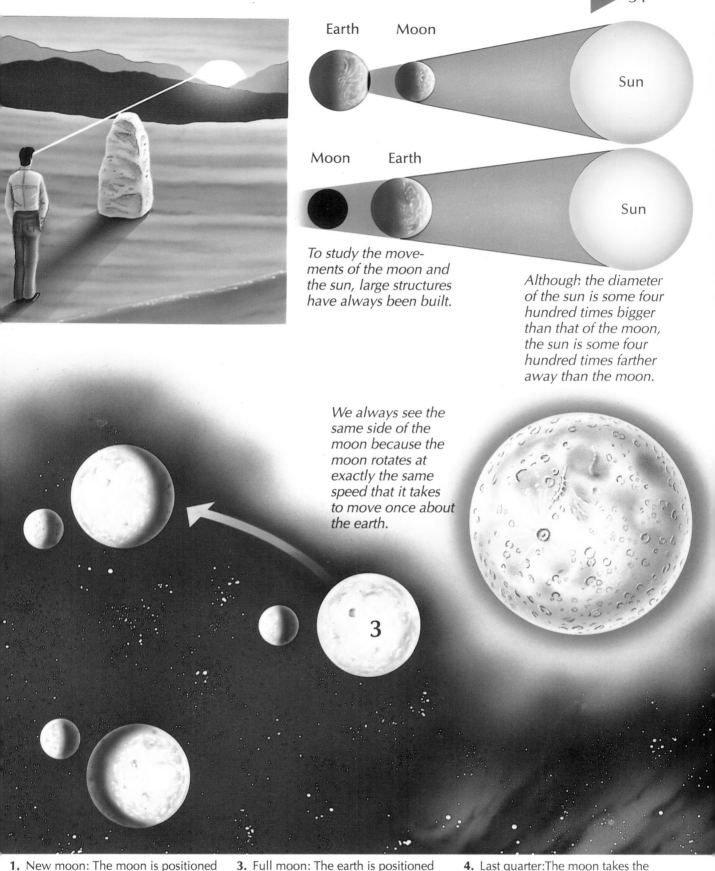

Earth   Moon

Sun

Moon   Earth

Sun

To study the movements of the moon and the sun, large structures have always been built.

Although the diameter of the sun is some four hundred times bigger than that of the moon, the sun is some four hundred times farther away than the moon.

We always see the same side of the moon because the moon rotates at exactly the same speed that it takes to move once about the earth.

1. New moon: The moon is positioned between the sun and the earth and we can see only its dark side.

2. First quarter: The illuminated part of the moon looks like a "D".

3. Full moon: The earth is positioned between the moon and the sun, and we can see the surface of the moon completely illuminated.

4. Last quarter: The moon takes the shape of a "C". Gradually, it begins to "shrink," and then narrows until it finally disappears.

Glossary

Deciduous plant: A plant that loses its leaves when the cold weather approaches.

Elliptical path: A flat, convex, and closed curve with two symmetrical axes that are perpendicular to each other. This is the type of path that the earth takes when it revolves around the sun.

Equinox: The period when the sun's path follows the equatorial line, and day and night are of equal length.

Fir trees (coniferous): Plants that have cones, such as pines, cypresses, and so on.

Leap year: A year that has 366 days because February has 29 days.

Perennial plants: Plants that keep their leaves all year round.

Photosynthesis: The process in which green plants compose organic matter from carbon dioxide by using light as a source of energy.

Pollination: The transportation or journey of the pollen from the anthers (masculine sexual organ of the plant) to the stigmas (female sexual organ of the plant). It can be transported by wind, insects, and so on.

Rotation: The movement of the earth on its own axis.

Satellite: A celestial body that orbits around a primary planet. For example, the moon is the earth's satellite.

Index